KU-032-564

Contents

Eat or be eaten!

All living things need energy to survive. Each day plants and animals must get enough food to give them the energy they need to carry on living.

Food chains

Animals spend a lot of their time either looking for food or trying to avoid being eaten themselves. A list of who eats who can be linked together to make a food chain.

A simple food chain will usually begin with a plant, because plants can make their own food from sunlight through a process called photosynthesis. The first link in the chain will be to an animal that eats the plant.

A herring gull is a top seashore predator, with nothing to fear from other creatures.

Yummy!

Some animals are 'scavengers', which means they eat the remains of dead animals and plants.

Who Eats Who?

1. plant

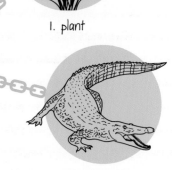

2. herbivore
(plant-eating animal)

3. carnivore
(meat-eating animal)

W
S
?

NORTHUMBERLAND COUNTY LIBRARY

Please return this book on or before the last date stamped below unless an extension of the loan period is granted.

Application for renewal may be made by letter or telephone.

Fines at the approved rate will be charged when a book is overdue.

FRANKLIN WATTS
LONDON • SYDNEY

This edition 2009

Copyright © 2005 Franklin Watts

Franklin Watts
338 Euston Road
London NW1 3BH

Franklin Watts Australia
Level 17/207 Kent Street
Sydney, NSW 2000

All rights reserved.

A CIP catalogue record for this book is
available from the British Library.

Dewey number: 577.69'9

ISBN 978 0 7496 8909 4

Printed in Malaysia

Franklin Watts is a division of
Hachette Children's books, an Hachette
Livre UK company.
www.hachettelivre.co.uk

Designer: Cali Roberts
Editor: Constance Novis
Art Director: Peter Scoulding
Editor-in-Chief: John C. Miles
Picture Research: Diana Morris
Artwork: Ian Thompson

Note to parents and teachers
Every effort has been made by the Publishers to ensure that the
websites in this book are suitable for children, that they are of
the highest educational value, and that they contain no inap-
propriate or offensive material. However, because of the
nature of the Internet, it is impossible to guarantee that the
contents of these sites will not be altered. We strongly advise
that Internet access is supervised by a responsible adult.

PICTURE CREDITS

Animals Animals/Oxford Scientific Photo Library: 4
Fred Breummer/Still Pictures: 19
Dave Fleetham/Oxford Scientific Photo Library: 9
Karen Gowlett-Holmes/Oxford Scientific Photo Library: 21
Jeff Greenberg/Still Pictures: 27
Al Grillo/Still Pictures: 26
Chinch Gryniewicz/Ecoscene: 5t, 5b
Martin Harvey/Still Pictures: 7, 25
Roger Jackman/Oxford Scientific Photo Library: 8
Steve Kauffman/Still Pictures: 14b
Paul Kay/Oxford Scientific Photo Library: 11
Colin Milkins/Oxford Scientific Photo Library: 13
Ted Miller/Still Pictures: 16
Oxford Scientific Photo Library: 10b, 12, 15, 20, 22
Jeffrey L. Rotman/Still Pictures: 24
Survival Anglia/Oxford Scientific Photo Library: 14t
Andrew Syred/SPL: 10t
Jochen Tach/Still Pictures: 6
Tom Vezo/Still Pictures: 23
Cal Vornberger/Still Pictures: front cover, 1, 18
Norbert Wu/Still Pictures: 17

*Every attempt has been made to clear copyright. Should
there be any inadvertent omission please apply to the
publisher for rectification.*

Food chain words

An animal that eats plants is called a herbivore. An animal that eats other animals is called a carnivore. An animal that eats both is called an omnivore.

An animal that hunts and kills other creatures is also called a predator. The last link in a food chain is usually to a top predator, an animal so powerful that it has nothing to fear from any other creature in its habitat.

We're in the chain!

Humans are omnivores, which means we eat both plants and animals. We are also the top predators in many food chains.

Seashore habitat

The Earth has many different natural regions, called habitats. A habitat, together with all the plants and animals that live there, is called an ecosystem.

The seashore is a unique ecosystem. The daily rise and fall of the tides means that it is underwater for part of the time. The plants and animals that live there have to be able to cope with the ever-changing conditions.

On most seashores, the tide rises and falls twice a day.

Chains become webs

On the seashore, like any other ecosystem, food chains often overlap with each other. A plant will often be eaten by many different animals and they, in turn, will be eaten by other creatures. These overlapping food chains can be linked together to make a food web, an overall picture of who eats whom at the seashore.

Tidal menu

The seashore is a very varied ecosystem, so its food web is complicated. Here both land and sea-based animals meet and feed according to the tides. There are predators on the seashore and in the water, too. The rise and fall of the tide controls which plants and animals are on the menu, and who will be there to dine!

We're in the chain!

Laver bread is a traditional Welsh food made from seaweed collected at low tide.

Crabs move between land and sea, looking for food.

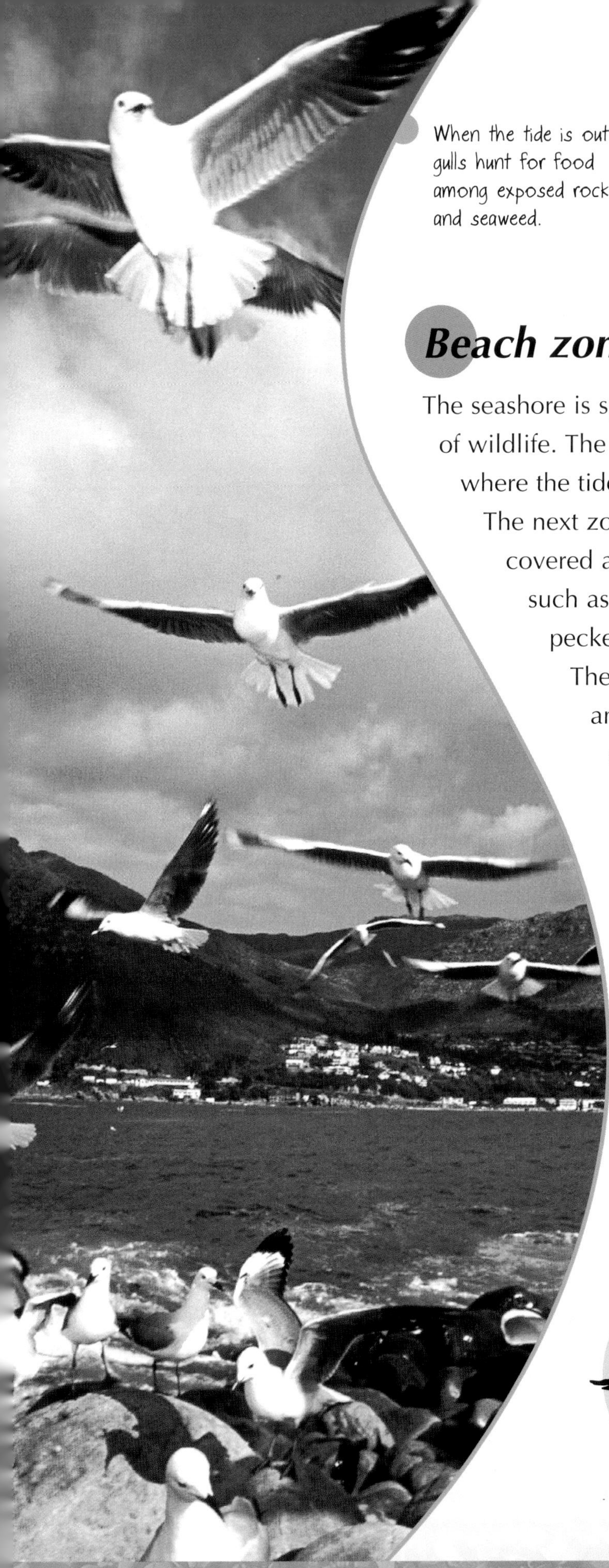

When the tide is out gulls hunt for food among exposed rocks and seaweed.

Yummy!

A limpet has a long rough tongue that it uses to scrape seaweed off rocks.

Beach zones

The seashore is split into zones, each with its own selection of wildlife. The highest zone is the 'splash zone', just above where the tide reaches. Here, salt-tolerant plants grow. The next zone down, the 'upper shore', is sometimes covered at high tide, and may be home to molluscs, such as limpets, which might be eaten by whelks or pecked off by seagulls when they are exposed. Then comes the middle shore, which is covered and uncovered every tide. The lower shore is only uncovered when the tide is very low. You might find small fish in the shallows here.

Who Eats Who?

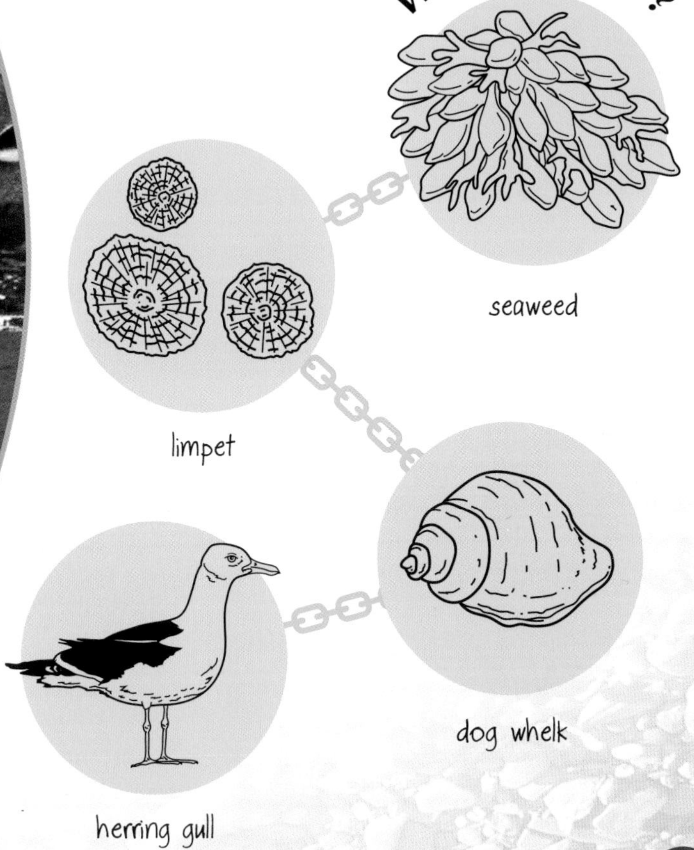

seaweed
limpet
dog whelk
herring gull

Starting the chain

Plants are at the bottom of every food chain because they provide food for others, but they eat nothing themselves. At the seashore the most common plant is seaweed.

Food for all

Plants form the basis of most food chains. Many different creatures graze on plants and themselves get eaten by others. Without plants, the animals at the top of the food chain would not survive, even though they might not eat plants themselves.

Plant of the sea

Seaweed is a type of plant called an algae. It does not have roots. Instead it absorbs everything it needs through its body cells. It does not flower either but, like all plants, it absorbs sunlight and uses this energy to create the food it needs to grow. This process is called photosynthesis. Inside seaweed cells there is a substance called chlorophyll that absorbs the sunlight.

Yummy!
Cows that graze on seaweed provide richer milk.

Two starfish rest on different types of seaweed.

This fish has evolved to look like the seaweed on which it lives, to confuse predators.

We're in the chain!

An extract of seaweed called carageenin is used in making many foods, such as cheese, ice cream toppings and puddings.

Seaweed starter

Seaweed can survive out of water for a short time between tides. It provides shelter and food for many insects, marine molluscs and fish fry (baby fish). At high tide, larger fish and crabs come to hunt among the dense seaweed fronds. At low tide birds come to feed on the creatures hiding among the seaweed that is exposed on the shore.

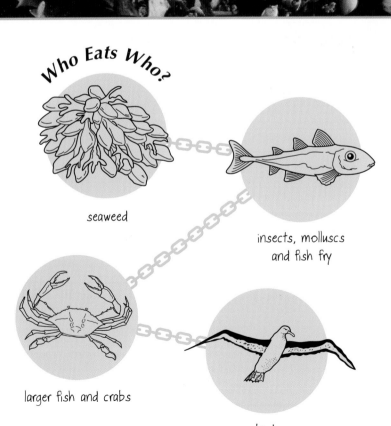

Who Eats Who?

seaweed

insects, molluscs and fish fry

larger fish and crabs

birds

Invisible eating

Tiny lifeforms called plankton are at the bottom of many seashore food chains. Plankton are so small they cannot be seen without a microscope.

A floating life

Some plankton are plants, called phytoplankton. Some are animals, called zooplankton. The smallest are no bigger than 1 micrometre in size (1 millionth of a metre). Plankton drift in sea currents alongside the seashore and in the open ocean.

Phytoplankton seen under a microscope.

Growing up

Many larger seashore creatures, such as barnacles and crabs, begin life as tiny zooplankton. If they avoid being eaten by others, they will gradually grow from as little as a 1000th of a millimetre across to full-size.

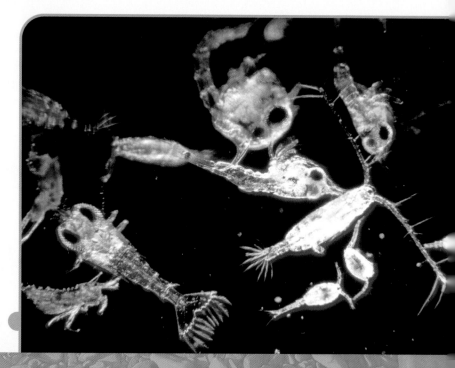

Magnified zooplankton.

Milky water

Plankton may be very small, but there are enormous numbers of them. In summer there can be so many of them that they can make the water look milky white. Others can form 'red tides' and produce toxins that poison other sea creatures.

A huge mass – a 'bloom' – of plankton has changed the colour of this seawater to red.

We're in the chain!

The food supply for plankton 'red tides' can come from sewage we pump into the sea.

Yummy!

Diatoms are some of the most numerous phytoplankton in the sea and they are eaten by lots of other creatures. They are covered with a 'skeleton' of silica, the same substance glass is made of.

Who Eats Who?

phytoplankton

zooplankton

prawn

human

Fixed for food

Many animals on land have to go looking for food, but there are a group of animals at the seashore that fix themselves to rocks and wait for the tides and currents to bring food to them.

Beach colonies

Mussels and barnacles attach themselves to rocks in large groups called colonies. Mussels have a bundle of tough threads called a beard that anchors them to the rock. When they are covered by the tide, they filter plankton from the seawater. When the tide goes out, they close their shells up tightly, trapping a little water inside to help them stay alive until the tide turns again.

We're in the chain!

Mussels are tasty to eat and many people collect them from seashore rocks. The tightly-closed shells open up when they are cooked.

A colony of mussels on a beach.

A dog whelk feeds on a mussel.

All about barnacles

A young barnacle glues itself on a rock headfirst and then forms a hard shell above itself. Its shell has two little door-like structures that open and shut, allowing its tiny legs to extend out and comb the water for plankton to eat.

Dogged driller

As mussels, barnacles and limpets are fixed to rocks they have to rely on their tough shells for protection, because they cannot escape from attackers. However, the dog whelk can bore through shells using a long tough body tube called a proboscis. When it has made a hole it sucks its meal out. It takes about three days to bore a hole.

Yummy!

A dog whelk lays about ten eggs. The ones that hatch first eat the others.

Who Eats Who?

plankton

mussel, limpet or barnacle

dog whelk

crab

Just visiting

Not all animals that feed at the seashore actually live there. Many animals just visit, often at the same time every year.

Turtle feast

In spring and summer, marine turtles come ashore to lay their eggs in the sand along the east coast of North America. Hungry raccoons visit the beaches to eat the eggs. Baby turtles that survive and hatch may get gobbled up by gulls before they are able to crawl to the sea. Even there they are not safe. Large fish such as sharks wait offshore to feed on them. Only a few turtles survive to adulthood. The surviving adult female turtles will return to the same beach to lay their own eggs.

A raccoon raids a turtle nest on a beach at night.

Seashore services

Many species of birds make long migrations every year to their winter or summer homes. Seashore mudflats and estuaries, with their rich source of food, are favourite places for migrating birds to rest and refuel before they continue their journey.

Migrating birds in the Sevem Estuary.

14

Who Eats Who?

turtle eggs and hatchlings

raccoon (for eggs)

shark (for hatchlings)

Yummy!

Estuaries are an incredibly rich source of food. Around half of the living things in the oceans are found eating and being eaten in estuaries.

We're in the chain!

People used to hunt turtles for their meat. The most prized part was the oily jelly-like layer between the turtle's body and its shell, which was used to flavour turtle soup.

Lion on the beach

On the Skeleton Coast of south-west Africa, the Namib desert reaches all the way down to the shore. Lions are occasional beach visitors here. They are sometimes spotted roaming the shoreline, looking for seals or stranded whales to eat.

A lion on the beach along the Skeleton Coast, Namibia.

Top predators

If you drew a seashore food web it would look like a pyramid. There would be lots of plants at the bottom, then small plant-eaters in the group above and then meat-eaters in the next group up. Above all of these there would be a few top predators.

What's on the menu?

Top predators don't always depend on just one type of food but will usually eat a variety of different creatures. They may have a favourite food, but they are usually adaptable and will eat whatever is on offer. This can often change with the seasons.

During the Alaskan summer, for instance, grizzly bears can be found hunting for food along the shore. They will forage for anything edible they can find, including fish, birds' eggs and shellfish.

A grizzly bear forages on an Alaskan shoreline.

Eat it up!

Large seabirds, such as gulls, are the most-common top predators on shorelines. The seashore is an ideal place for them because they eat so many different things. They feed on fish, shellfish and molluscs, and will also take the chicks and eggs of other birds. They scavenge on dead creatures washed up on the seashore as well and even steal picnic food from human sunbathers!

A shark grabs an albatross chick near the shore of the Hawaiian islands.

Yummy!

Many seabirds feed their young with partly digested food. Parent birds regurgitate the food as a sort of thick fish soup straight into the chick's open mouth.

Watch out, sharks about

A fearsome top predator appears in July along the shorelines of the north-west Hawaiian islands. At this time of year albatross chicks are learning to fly and feed for themselves. They float on the water near the shore, but in the shallows tiger sharks lie in wait to gobble them up.

Who Eats Who?

plankton

fish

albatross/albatross chicks

tiger shark

Clearing up

All plants and animals die eventually, but that does not mean they are lost to the seashore food web. Some creatures scavenge, which means they eat dead material, helping to recycle it back into the food chain.

Top scavengers

Some top predators, such as seagulls, scavenge the bodies of dead sea creatures washed up on the beach. The birds have very powerful beaks that they use to rip off pieces of flesh and bone.

Scavengers from the sea

When the tide comes in to the seashore, crabs come with it. They are very good scavengers, using their powerful pincers and claw-like mouthparts to eat dead creatures, and so help to clear up the shore. Once they return to the sea they might get eaten by lobsters, who might in turn be eaten by an octopus!

A close-up of a seagull's beak.

Who Eats Who?

dead fish

crab

lobster

octopus

Crabs scavenge on a dead crab.

Picking up the pieces

As the remains of a dead plant or animal are broken up by scavengers, tiny fragments float off in the water. This is called detritus. Many seashore creatures depend on this food source, including little shell-covered creatures called cockles that live in the sand. A cockle sucks up the sand via a small tube, filters out the food particles trapped in it and then pushes the sand out again.

Rockpool dwellers

Seashore rockpools are full of plant and animal life. The creatures that live there must be able to survive if their pool dries out before the next tide fills it with water again.

Rockpool hunters

Anemones are often found in rockpools. They look a little like flowers, but they are actually predatory animals. They have tentacles lined with stinging cells that they use to kill small fish that swim too close. If a beadlet anemone is left out of the water when the tide goes out, it will tuck its tentacles inside its body to protect itself from drying out until the water returns.

Yummy!

The starfish uses its strong arms to pull shells apart and get to the soft creatures inside. Then it pushes its stomach into the hole to digest its prey.

An anemone traps a fish with its tentacles.

An urchin
uses seaweed
fronds as camouflage.

Starfish and sea urchins

Starfish hunt for shelled creatures, such
as mussels. They have tiny tube feet along
each arm that they use to move around to
help open up their prey. Sea urchins also
move around on tube feet and use them to
pick up bits of seaweed to attach to their
spines, disguising themselves from
hungry fish.

Danger zone

At low tide, animals in the rockpool
are exposed to the danger of hunting
birds. For instance, the oystercatcher
can use its strong pointed beak to
knock limpets and mussels off the
rocks. Crabs and starfish take refuge
under rocks or seaweed, waiting for the
sea to return before they venture out.

Who Eats Who?

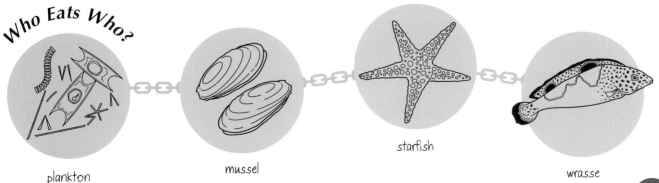

plankton   mussel   starfish   wrasse

Under the sand

Beaches and mudflats that are exposed at low tide may seem empty, but in fact they teem with hidden life.

Out of sight

Many small animals hide underneath the sand or mud. That way they avoid drying out at low tide, and keep themselves away from hungry enemies. Lugworms live in U-shaped burrows in the sand. They filter out food particles from the sand then push the filtered sand out through a long tube, making little sandpiles on the surface above.

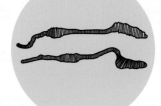

detritus in the sand

lugworm

oystercatcher

A sand pile made by a lugworm hiding under the surface of a beach.

22

Mini beach beasts

Sand hoppers are small relatives of shrimp. They bury themselves in the sand or in among seaweed during the day, to hide from hungry fish, crabs and seabirds. They come out mostly at night to feed on decaying food brought in by the tide. You might see them jumping around if you disturb some seaweed.

No hiding place

Many wading birds have specialised beaks for hunting prey along the seashore. Godwits and sanderlings use their long, thin beaks to probe the sand and mud looking for juicy worms to eat. Turnstones use their short stout bills to turn over stones and seaweed in their search for food.

Sanderlings search for food on estuary mudflats.

Yummy!

Giant beach worms 2.5m long live under the sand on the beaches of eastern Australia. Fishermen pull them out to make fishing bait.

We're in the chain!

People who live by estuaries sometimes harvest cockles and clams from exposed mudflats.

Swampy shore

Not all seashores are sandy or rocky. In very warm climates, mangrove swamps may grow alongside the sea edge. These places have their own unique food webs.

Tidal tree food

Mangrove trees provide both food and protection. When the tide goes out fiddler crabs emerge from their mud burrows to feed on the remains of mangrove leaves that have dropped on to the mud. When the tide is in, small fish shelter from bigger predators in the tangled mangrove roots. In Queensland, Australia, these predators include fearsome saltwater crocodiles that come in with the tide.

We're in the chain!
Saltwater crocodiles are extremely ferocious and will eat humans, given the chance.

A saltwater crocodile in a coastal mangrove swamp.

In or out

Mudskipper fish live among mangrove swamps in Africa and Australia. They are at home in the sea, like any other fish, but they can breathe on land as long as they keep their gills moist. They use their fins like legs to pull themselves along, to burrow in the mud or even climb the mangrove roots. Baby saltwater crocodiles and fish-eating birds, such as herons, are their main enemies.

Yummy!

Among other things, big mudskippers will sometimes eat smaller ones.

mudskipper

saltwater crocodile

Who Eats Who?

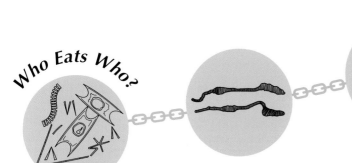

plankton

worms/crustaceans

mudskipper

A mudskipper peers across an Australian swamp.

25

Breaking the chains

A food chain depends on all of its links staying strong. If any of the links are weakened or broken, it affects each of the other links in the chain, and the overall food web.

Problems from humans

Some of the biggest risks to seashore food chains come from the activities of humans. When the giant oil tanker *Exxon Valdez* ran aground in Prince William Sound in Alaska in 1989, it spilled a huge quantity of oil into the surrounding bays. Many living things at all levels of the food web were killed as a result.

Rebuilding slowly

Fortunately the seaweed in the area recovered quite quickly after the *Exxon Valdez* disaster. As a result, animals that depend on the seaweed for food have also recovered well. Other creatures have been less lucky. Many mussel beds are still contaminated, so animals that eat mussels are taking much longer to return in any numbers.

Cleaning up after the *Exxon Valdez* disaster, 1989.

Poisoning of a food chain

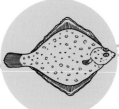

plankton swim in polluted water

fish absorb pollution into their bodies

seals, whales and humans eat the poisoned fish

Turtle hatchlings and holidaymakers share a crowded beach. The nesting area has been roped off to protect it.

We're in the chain!

Scientists think that in many parts of the world fish stocks are in danger from people over-fishing. It's even possible that the oceans will one day end up like barren deserts with little life.

Holiday damage

Even holidaymakers can bring about the destruction of a habitat and the breaking of its food chains. Some turtle species are close to extinction because their nest sites have been disrupted by beachside holiday developments. Their eggs are crushed by humans using the beach, and the lights on the buildings confuse the baby hatchlings, which start to crawl the wrong way and never make it to the sea. Animals that feed on the turtles are also badly affected because they have less food.

Food web

Here is an example of who eats who in a seashore food web. Surrounding it are some fascinating seashore facts.

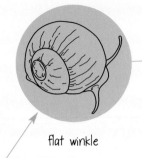
flat winkle

The world's tiniest starfish, the asterinid sea star, is found on the coast of South Australia. It measures about 9 mm across.

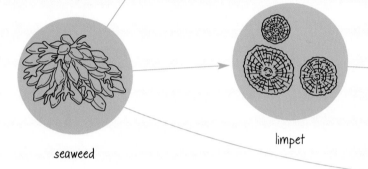
seaweed

limpet

A herring gull can drink sea-water as well as fresh water. It has special glands that allow it to get rid of the salt through its nose.

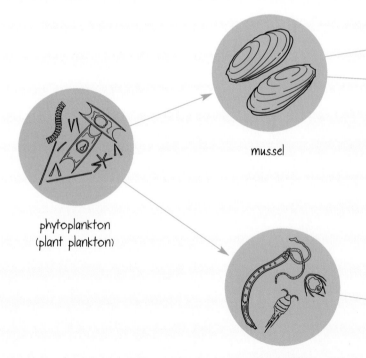
phytoplankton (plant plankton)

mussel

zooplankton (animal plankton)

In one of the world's worst pollution accidents the *Exxon Valdez* dropped 11 million gallons of oil into the sea, killing an estimated 250,000 seabirds.

Limpets change sex as they get older, from male to female.

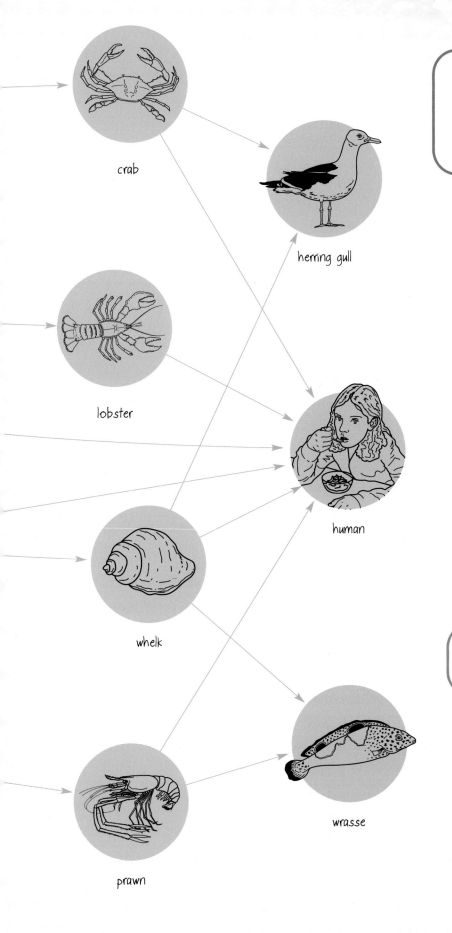

crab

herring gull

lobster

human

whelk

wrasse

prawn

Mangrove seedlings can survive floating for up to 1,600 km in the sea, and still take root when they reach land.

In the Bay of Fundy, between Canada and eastern USA, tides can rise and fall up to 14.5 m, the biggest amount anywhere in the world.

Mangrove trees can survive in water ten times more salty than other plants can.

An oystercatcher's favourite food is not oysters, but mussels.

The dog whelk population has been cut by the polluting effects of ship's paint. It makes the dog whelks infertile.

Glossary

algae

simple plants that do not have flowers, such as seaweed.

bivalve mollusc

a creature with a two-part shell, hinged together in the middle.

carnivore

an animal that eats only meat.

crustacean

a type of water animal with an exoskeleton (a skeleton on the outside of its body).

detritus

tiny particles of dead animal and plant-material.

ecosystem

a community of living things and their physical environment.

estuary

the mouth of a river where it runs into the sea.

food chain

the feeding links between plants and animals showing who eats whom.

food web

a map of all the feeding links in a habitat, showing how the plants and animals are connected to each other.

herbivore

an animal that eats only plants.

high water

the highest point the tide reaches on a seashore before it starts to go back down.

mangrove tree

a type of tree that can survive in salty tidal water.

low water

the lowest point a tide reaches on a seashore before it starts to come back up.

migration

the journey of an animal between one area and another, to find better living conditions.

mollusc

a soft-bodied animal, usually with a hard shell.

mudflat

a stretch of mud alongside a river or a seashore.

omnivore

a creature that eats both plants and meat.

photosynthesis

the process by which plants capture the energy of sunlight to make sugar into food.

plankton

microscopic plants and animals that live in water: phytoplankton are plants and zooplankton are tiny animals.

scavenger

an animal that feeds off the remains of dead creatures and plants.

splash zone

the area on the shore above high tide that gets sprayed by the waves.

tentacles

long flexible feelers, sometimes with stinging cells or suckers on them.

tide

the daily rise and fall of the sea.

Seashore Websites

www.mobot.org/salt/sandy/indexfr.htm

Information about different kinds of seashore.

www.theseashore.org.uk

Understand the seashore and seashore life.

www.seashells.org

Information about identifying and preserving seashells you find on the beach.

www.bbc.co.uk/nature/blueplanet/edge

Play seashore games and take seashore challenges.

www.nps.gov/calo/kids.htm

Learn about seashore plants, shells, birds and sealife.

Index